# JUMP-STARTING A CAREER IN

# PHARMACEUTICALS

TAMRA B. ORR

ROSEN
PUBLISHING®

New York

Published in 2014 by The Rosen Publishing Group, Inc.
29 East 21st Street, New York, NY 10010

**Library of Congress Cataloging-in-Publication Data**

Orr, Tamra.
Jump-starting a career in pharmaceuticals/Tamra B. Orr.—First edition.
    pages cm.—(Health care careers in 2 years)
Includes bibliographical references and index.
ISBN 978-1-4777-1693-9 (library binding)
1. Pharmacy technicians—Vocational guidance. 2. Pharmacy—Vocational guidance. I. Title.
RS122.95.O77 2014
615.1023—dc23

                                                          2013013752


*Manufactured in Malaysia*

CPSIA Compliance Information: Batch #W14YA: For further information, contact Rosen Publishing, New York, New York, at 1-800-237-9932.

# CONTENTS

# INTRODUCTION

The day begins as you walk in the back door of the pharmacy and slide your arms out of your jacket and into your white lab coat. Already you feel professional and ready to take on whatever the day might send your way.

While some mornings you get the chance to catch up with coworkers, including the head pharmacist, today is not one of those days. A particularly harsh strain of the winter flu has been steamrolling its way through your community, and the long line at the pharmacy counter is all the proof you need that it is still raging. Typically, the morning hours begin with a trickle of patients, but today you can see at least eight standing in line already. There are four cars waiting in the drive-up, and the phone doesn't seem to stop ringing. Welcome to a busy day for the typical pharmacy technician!

The morning speeds by as you accept prescriptions in person from patients, as well as over the phone from physicians. A quick check of the fax machine turns up several more medical orders. Most of these are to help people deal with the annoying symptoms of this stubborn flu virus. As you have learned while training for this job, decongestants help with the sinus congestion of flu. Expectorants help with coughing. Analgesics mitigate the discomfort of muscle aches and keep the fever from climbing too high or too fast.

Being part of the pharmacy team gives you the opportunity to help others feel better, heal faster, and live longer.

You spend the day measuring liquids, counting pills, checking dosages, verifying prescriptions, ordering refills, and typing and affixing labels. At last, the line of patients is almost gone, but not for long. Soon enough, your "regulars" meander in, customers who come in often enough that you have had a chance to get to know them. As you fill Mrs. Connors's prescription for her high blood pressure medication, you get caught up on how her grandson is doing in college. Mr. Ellis keeps you up to date on his latest golf score as he gets a refill for his acid reflux medication. Caroline Johnson tells you about her upcoming job interview as you refill her asthma medication.

Most of the patients who come in are friendly and personable, but some are quiet. Some are clearly worried or even frightened. Most have questions, which you efficiently refer to the pharmacist. You remember to deal with these patients with compassion and confidence as you dispense some peace of mind along with the medications. When the day is done, you know you've done your job well. You filled prescriptions, helped your coworkers, reassured and listened to patients, and kept up with requests. It was a good day overall.

Does this type of day sound exciting? Does it sound like something you would like to do? It can be, with some time, effort, and interest. While many careers in pharmaceuticals require a bachelor's, master's, or even doctorate degree, becoming a pharmacy technician, a pharmaceutical manufacturing technician, a quality control associate, a process technician, a pharmaceutical sales representative, a pharmacy billing specialist, a pharmacy records manager, or a pharmacy clerk takes only two years or less to achieve.

If these pathways appeal to you, start doing your homework now. Make sure you do well in all of your science and math classes, as these will form the foundation for work in any part of the pharmaceutical field. If you have the opportunity to take extra classes in high school, do so. If honors or college-prep classes are an option, take those as well. Once you graduate from high school, research your options: on-the-job training, certification, or an associate's degree? An online program, community college, or traditional school? Stop by your neighborhood Walgreens, Rite Aid, CVS, or other drugstore and ask a few questions if the pharmacy department is not busy. Do the same at local hospitals, nursing homes, or clinics.

A great career is just around the corner, so take the time to learn more about it. A good day in the pharmaceutical industry may certainly be in your very near future.

# Chapter 1

# On the Pharm Tech Track

**H**ow many times have you been asked in the last few months what you plan to do with the rest of your life? It's a common question as high school graduation looms closer and closer. It is highly likely that family, friends, teachers, and coworkers will begin to ask about your future plans. But deciding what profession suits you, which direction to go in, and what steps to take next is tough.

Decisions, decisions. Trying to choose what career pathway to take is never easy. After all, how can you be sure what jobs fit your personality, experience, and interests? Even if you can pinpoint those answers, how much will the job pay? How much training and education will it require? How much will that cost?

Many young people find themselves looking into a career within the health or medical fields. These are rapidly growing professions, and there are many different possible positions within them. A number of those fields require four, six, or even more years of college and graduate work to enter. Is it possible to find a position in the health care industry with only a two-year associate's degree, certification, or even less? The short answer is… yes! In the pharmaceutical field, you can get a job as a pharmacy technician, pharmaceutical manufacturing technician, quality control associate, process technician, pharmaceutical sales representative, pharmacy billing specialist, pharmacy records manager, or pharmacy clerk in two years or less.

## A Successful Industry

The pharmaceutical business is booming, to put it mildly! It is one of the fastest-growing industries in the entire country. In 2008, it reported a $773 billion profit! As the number of senior citizens in the United States continues to climb, the need for additional medications to treat and even slow down the aging process will rise as well. As diseases like AIDS, HIV, hepatitis, cancer, and diabetes continue to afflict millions of people, the need for prescriptions to control, and perhaps one day even cure, these illnesses will grow.

It is important to note, however, that as successful and profitable as the pharmaceutical business is, it is also one of the most heavily regulated. It takes twelve to fifteen years and an astounding $1.7 billion for a drug to go from being discovered to being put on the market. The reason the process is so incredibly slow is the testing and regulatory process. The U.S. Food and Drug Administration (FDA) oversees every single step in order to protect all future patients from harm. While this is necessary for safety purposes, it also makes the process much more complicated.

Getting involved in the pharmaceutical industry can be a very smart step to make! The U.S. Bureau of Labor Statistics (BLS) reports that, nationwide, the position of

As more and more Americans are aging, the need for medication—and the people who produce and dispense it—grows.

pharmacy tech—one of the most popular and rewarding two-year career paths within the pharmaceutical field—is growing at more than 30 percent a year. This is far, far faster than the average growth rate for other careers. With such a steady growth rate, job openings will most likely be found throughout the entire country.

## Undergoing Change

Let's examine the pharmacy tech position more closely. It is undergoing some distinct changes. In the past, students could frequently get hired with nothing more than a GED or high school diploma. Over time, however, that has changed. Currently, the vast majority of states require techs to either be certified or have a two-year associate of science (AS) or associate in applied science (AAS) degree. In turn, this requirement has resulted in an increasing number of colleges offering two-year programs.

The training offered to become a pharmacy tech (also referred to as a pharmacy assistant) varies from one school to the next. Some programs last six months, resulting in a certificate or diploma, while some last twenty-four months and result in an associate's degree. To find out the requirements in your state, contact the state board of pharmacy. In addition to training, applicants must agree to a criminal background check and take an official exam. Schools report that those applicants with two-year degrees are hired first and tend to earn a higher hourly rate. In other words, the more education you get, the better your job opportunities.

## Tech Traits

Is being a pharmacy technician a good match for you? Here are some of the basic traits, abilities, and skills experts believe you need to have to succeed in the field:

- Ability to stand for long periods of time
- Well-organized
- Follow instructions
- Empathetic
- Strong interpersonal skills
- Familiarity with computers

- Dependable
- Accurate and precise
- Good time management skills
- Detail-oriented
- Proficient at multitasking
- Experience in customer service
- Able to work both independently and collaboratively
- Strong math, reading, spelling, and conversational skills
- Ability to deal with sick, angry, worried, and impatient customers

Does that sound like you? If you think the idea of working with medicine and helping people who are sick or in pain sounds like the right pathway for you, explore becoming a pharmacy technician. It may just be the perfect choice. And it will give you a great answer to give all those family, friends, and teachers who keep asking you, "So, what do you plan to do after graduation?"

## Daily Duties

Where you work will determine not only your pay rate and scheduled hours, but also what responsibilities you may be given. For example, if you're a tech in a retail store, you may be ringing up products at the cash register. If you work in a nursing home facility, however, you may be walking into patients' rooms to deliver medication. Keep that in mind as you read through the list of general pharmacy tech duties. Typically, you will:

- Be given prescriptions to read, fill, and process. It is your responsibility to verify the information about the doctor and patient and ensure that the dosage is accurate. It is the pharmacist's duty to check your work and make sure the proper medication is given out.
- Learn the rules and apply them to maintain proper storage and security conditions for all medications.
- Answer the phone to take refill requests.
- Fill bottles with the prescribed medications.
- Type and affix labels with accurate information.
- Assist customers with simple questions and refer medication or medical questions to the available pharmacist.
- Price and file prescriptions.
- Clean and maintain basic equipment and work areas, including sterilizing glassware.
- Establish and maintain patient profiles, including lists of medications.
- Order, label, and count stocks of medications, chemicals, and supplies.
- Enter inventory results into the computer's database.
- Record and store incoming supplies, including verifying quantities delivered against invoices and informing supervisors of stock needs or shortages.
- Promote drug compliance (carefully following directions regarding drug usage) with patients.
- Report any adverse reactions or side effects to pharmacists.

- Transfer medications from vials to sterile syringes.
- Add measured drugs to intravenous (IV) solutions.
- Supply and monitor robotic machines that dispense medication into containers.
- Prepare and process medical insurance claim forms and records.
- Mix pharmaceutical preparations according to the prescriptions.
- Operate the cash register to process payments from patients.
- Deliver medications and pharmaceutical supplies to patients in nursing homes.
- Price stock and mark items for sale.

Attention to detail is an essential skill for pharmacy technicians to develop, as it will play a role in virtually every one of your daily responsibilities.

Don't be overwhelmed by this list. It may sound like more work than you can possibly do, but remember, all new jobs that you have ever had looked that way at first. Remember learning to drive a car and seeing the list of everything you have to pay attention to? Mirrors, traffic, speed limit, street signs, weather hazards, and directions, just to name a few. It seemed absolutely impossible, and now you juggle all of it automatically every time you get behind the wheel.

## Location, Location, Location

Pharmacy technicians may find themselves working in a variety of locations. According to the Bureau of Labor Statistics, just over half of today's pharmacy techs work in pharmacies. Seven percent work in grocery stores, like Safeway, or drugstores, like Walgreens, CVS, or Rite Aid. A mere 5 percent work in department stores, such as Walmart. The rest are employed in a variety of places including:

- Hospitals
- Nursing homes
- Insurance companies
- Military base pharmacies
- Long-term care facilities
- Mail service pharmacies
- Specialty compounding pharmacies
- Home health care/home infusion pharmacies
- Pharmacy benefit management companies
- Nuclear medicine pharmacies
- Clinic pharmacies

Where you work as a pharmacy technician will determine your pay rate, weekly hours, and responsibilities. In some locations you will work primarily with physicians,

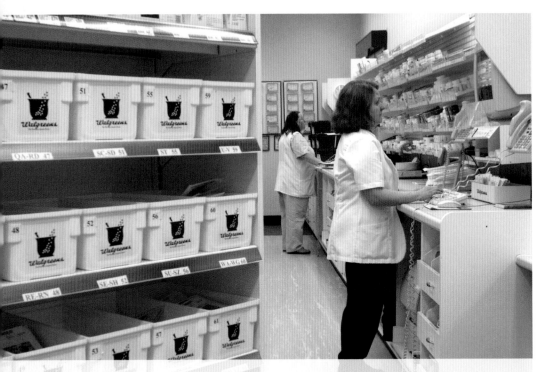

Many pharmacy technicians are found behind the counters of familiar chain drugstores, such as Walgreens, Rite Aid, and CVS.

while in others you might be interacting primarily with patients. You might be ringing up a package of diapers or a bottle of shampoo along with the prescriptions.

Here are some other things to keep in mind about which location you want to work in:

- If you work in a hospital, you will most likely work a variety of shifts because these facilities are open 24/7. You will mainly work directly with doctors.

# A CLOSER LOOK

Shannon Ydoyaga, interim director of the Health Careers Resource Center for the Dallas County Community College District (DCCCD) in Texas, knows a great deal about health degrees and where they can lead students. DCCCD's Health Careers Resource Center is designed for students who have chosen to pursue a health care field or just need guidance in order to make that choice. The college offers courses in nursing, sonography, radiologic sciences, emergency medical services, and, of course, pharmacy technology.

Ydoyaga has some simple and helpful advice for young people considering a career as a pharmacy tech. "You need to have strong math skills, in addition to great customer service capabilities," she advises. "Pharmaceutical positions learn about the top two hundred drugs and adverse reactions that may occur within patients when taking several types of medications. Students should also have an interest in human diseases and how these are treated.

"Programs for pharmacy technicians can help students to work in retail, assisted living, or hospital settings, or to prepare for a doctor of pharmacy program through a university," she continues. "The training can also be beneficial for individuals interested in pharmaceutical sales." In addition, according to Ydoyaga, students should be interested in research, as new medications and diseases are being found daily.

- If you work in a long-term care facility, you will provide medications only for the patients living in that specific facility and have very little customer interaction.
- If you work in a drugstore or a retail pharmacy, you will commonly talk to and interact with customers. Answering phones and ringing up sales are typical duties.
- If you work for an insurance company, you will spend far less time working with patients or handling prescriptions and far more time making your way through piles of paperwork, including denial and approval letters, claims, and data reports.

## *Advice from an Expert*

LiAnne Webster is the health professions administrator for the pharmacy technician program at Richland College in Dallas, Texas. She was a pharmacy tech herself for fifteen years and a pharmacy technician supervisor for an additional three years. Today, she administers the school's pharmacy technician certificate program.

Webster says that students pursuing this field should have a strong interest in helping people, as well as in protecting patient health and safety. "Mathematics skills, up to the college math level, are critical to being able to perform medication dosage calculation. They are also critical to the protection of patient safety, as the miscalculation of a dose may result in harm to a patient," explains Webster. "Students who have taken college-level biology, anatomy/physiology, or chemistry will be in a good position to perform well in this career, and strong oral and written communication skills are also very important."

Webster points out that now all pharmacy technician programs require two years of study. The training is not limited to pharmacy tech jobs either. "Credit programs usually result in an associate in applied science (AAS) degree," she says. "Pharmacy technicians may wish to seek positions as pharmaceutical sales representatives with an undergraduate degree and may be able to seek nonclinical management positions in both retail and hospital pharmacy settings. Pharmacy technicians may further choose to continue their education to seek professional degrees such as doctor of pharmacy (PharmD) or master's in pharmaceutical science for research and development.

All of those high-level math classes you took in high school or community college will serve you well if you pursue a career as a pharmacy tech.

Experienced and credentialed pharmacy technicians may choose to go to a community college or other institution of higher education to become pharmacy technician educators," she adds.

"The pharmacy technician career path is one in which there are a variety of opportunities in a field that is very stable and growing all over the country," Webster continues. "While most states do not require formal education, individuals place themselves in the best position for success in the profession and on the certification exam by attending a training program prior to entering practice. This is NOT a career for a person to get into just because the entry-level pay is decent," she emphasizes. "Pharmacy technician practice is patient care–driven, and those who wish to engage this profession must recognize this as the most important aspect of their jobs.

"Further, those who wish to further engage their profession should also strongly consider giving back to that profession through involvement in pharmacy professional organizations. Not only will that allow them to gain the continuing education credit required to maintain their professional credentials [requirements range between twenty and forty continuing education credit hours every one to two years, varying by state], but also allows technicians to have a voice within organizations that appeal to lawmakers concerning legislation that impacts the profession of pharmacy."

# Chapter 2

# Tech Training

an you get a pharmacy technician job with nothing more than a high school diploma or a GED? Yes . . . and no. Yes, you may be able to get hired directly from high school, without any formal training, but that may not be true for much longer.

According to the National Association of Boards of Pharmacy's 2013 Survey of Pharmacy Law, 80 percent of states require some type of training to earn this job. Eighteen states require professional certification. Research has shown that the more training you receive, the faster you will be hired and the more money you will earn. On-the-job training often lasts from three months to a year. Diploma and certification programs take six to twelve months to complete. An associate's degree requires two years. A number of chain drugstores, such as Walgreens and CVS, may offer on-the-job training for their pharmacy technicians. Once this training is completed, you will be asked to take the national Pharmacy Technician Certification Board (PTCB) exam. Usually, your employer will pay the exam fee.

## *Tech Coursework*

What classes will you typically take for pharmacy tech training? It may change slightly from one college to the next, but here are the primary courses:

### General education classes: twenty credit hours

- Mathematics for the health sciences
- Speech communication
- Applied composition or English composition
- General psychology

A strong interest in science will make studying and preparing for a career as a pharmacy tech a highly stimulating and enjoyable experience.

## Pharmacy technician requirements: seventy-five credit hours

- Pharmacy technician fundamentals and ethics
- Pharmacology I
- Top 200 drugs I
- Pharmacology II
- Outpatient pharmacy preparations and record-keeping I
- Outpatient pharmacy preparations and record-keeping II
- Intravenous (IV) admixture advanced techniques
- Inpatient and home health care pharmacy preparations and recordkeeping
- Top 200 drugs II
- Medical terminology/anatomy and physiology for pharmacy technicians I
- Pharmacy law and references I
- Chemistry for pharmacy
- Business office machines I
- Business office machines II
- Business office machines III
- Medical terminology/anatomy and physiology for technicians II
- Pharmacy law and references II
- Pharmacy calculations
- Communications and customer service
- Management, supervision, and human relations
- Pharmacy practice internship I
- Pharmacy practice internship II

## Choosing a Program

How do you know which pharmacy technician program to choose? Start by asking the following questions:

1. Does the list of courses cover the different areas of pharmacy work?

Studying chemistry and logging practical time in laboratories will greatly enhance your credentials when applying for work as a pharmacy technician.

2. Will graduates have the educational foundation they need to pursue career advancement?
3. Does the program emphasize preparation for the Pharmacy Technician Certification Board (PTCB) exam?
4. Are classes small enough for a strong learning environment?
5. Does the school offer plenty of supervised practical experience in an actual pharmacy setting?
6. What percentage of the school's graduates are hired?
7. Does the school offer any kind of job placement or internships?
8. Are there financial aid options, including scholarships, student loans, and grants?

9. How close is the school to where you live or work? The closer it is, the more convenient it is to get to and from.
10. How much does the program cost? Typically, schools charge by the credit, and pharmacy tech programs range from thirty-six to ninety-five credits. The cost per credit varies greatly, but $200 is the average amount.

Decisions about your education should never be taken lightly or without a good deal of thought, regardless of what field you choose. If you decide that a career in pharmaceuticals is the best choice, a pharmacy technician job can be a great start. It can help you decide if this is an area you want to pursue further or use as a jump-start to another career entirely.

## Passing the Test

Whether you decide to get on-the-job training, earn a certificate, or pursue a full associate's degree, you will end up having to take the Pharmacy Technician Certification Board exam. Knowing what will be on the test will make it easier for you to study and prepare.

The PTCB exam is a nationally accredited certification exam. In order to take it, you have to meet several basic requirements:

- Be at least eighteen years old
- Have a high school diploma or GED
- Have no felony convictions

# SAMPLE TEST QUESTIONS

Wondering how well you would do on a PTCB exam? Check out these sample questions and see if you know the answers. If not, don't worry! You will know them after taking the appropriate courses and studying for the exam.

**1. In a professional pharmacy setting, which agency regulates the majority of pharmacy technician activities and practices?**

A.Food and Drug Administration
B.State Board of Pharmacy
C.Drug Enforcement Agency
D.Pharmacy Technician Certification Board

**2. For which of the following would a patient be prescribed an albuterol inhaler?**

A.Hypertension
B.Asthma
C.Smoking cessation
D.Post myocardial infarction

**3. Which of the following are not treated with barbiturates?**

A.Seizures
B.Hypotension
C.Insomnia
D.Anxiety

**4. Which of the following drugs is associated with drug-induced hepatitis?**
A. Valproic acid
B. Quinidine
C. Isoniazid
D. Ethosuximide

**5. A drug ending in the suffix –navir is considered a _____.**
A. Antidepressant
B. Protease inhibitor
C. Beta antagonist
D. H2 antagonist

Answer key: (1) C; (2) C; (3) B; (4) C; (5) B

- Have no drug- or pharmacy-related convictions
- Have no denial, suspension, or restrictions from the state board of pharmacy

What is on the PTCB test? It is made up of ninety multiple-choice questions and is divided into three parts:

- Sixty-six percent of the test involves questions regarding assisting the pharmacist in serving patients.
- Twenty-two percent of the test involves questions regarding maintaining medication and inventory control systems.

- Twelve percent of the test involves questions regarding participating in the administration and management of pharmacy practice.

You have 110 minutes (1 hour and 50 minutes) to complete the exam. There is a five-minute tutorial at the beginning of the test, and a five-minute survey at the end, for a total test time of two hours. Ten of the ninety questions will not figure into your score. These questions are being piloted or tested for future versions of the test. Of course, you will not know which ten they are, so you need to answer all ninety questions. To pass the test, you have to score at least 650 out of 900 possible points. Results are available immediately, with a pass-fail notice on the computer and printout of all exam results. What happens if you don't score 650? You have the chance to take the exam two more times.

The cost of the PTCB exam is currently $129. Often your employer will pay this fee for you. After you have passed the test, you are officially declared a certified pharmacy technician, or CPhT. You will remain certified for two years. After two years have passed, you will need to take continuing education courses in order to renew your certification.

# Chapter 3

# Making Medicine

**P**erhaps you are far more interested in producing and testing medications than dispensing and handing them out? Pharmaceutical manufacturing and biomanufacturing—the production, isolation, and purification of drugs and medicines—is one of the pathways open to those interested in a career in the pharmaceutical industry. Despite the high-tech nature of the work, you do not need an advanced degree to get started in the field. For example, in the state of North Carolina, 67 percent of employees in pharmaceutical manufacturing and biomanufacturing are trained at the community college level or less.

For entry-level employment training, individuals can enter associate in applied science (AAS) programs. These degree programs offer practical, job-oriented training in science and technology. In addition, life science degree programs offer employment opportunities in areas ranging from agricultural biotechnology and bioprocess technology to marine technology and many other options. AAS degree programs can typically be completed by full-time students in two years. Course work includes general core

Jobs within pharmaceutical factories are often a great gateway to more advanced positions in drug manufacturing and quality control.

courses as well as classes in mathematics, natural sciences, and computer science. Upon completion of the AAS degree, if students wish to continue their education rather than immediately seek employment, their course work may be accepted by a four-year college or university for transfer credit in a related field.

Some schools offer a biopharmaceutical technology curriculum designed to prepare students for employment in pharmaceutical manufacturing and related industries. Major emphasis is placed on manufacturing processes, quality control and quality assurance procedures, and research and development. Course work includes general education, computer applications, biology, chemistry, industrial safety, and pharmaceutical-specific classes. Upon graduation, students should qualify for numerous positions within the industry. These include chemical quality assurance, microbiological quality assurance, product inspection, documentation review, manufacturing, and product/process validation.

## Pharmaceutical and Medicine Manufacturing Science Technician

One of the job titles that awaits graduates is pharmaceutical and medicine manufacturing science technician. These technicians are responsible for the production of all the medicines available for patient use today, including over-the-counter and prescription medications. In addition to creating treatment medications, pharmaceutical and medicine manufacturing science technicians also help make preventative medicines, such as flu and tetanus vaccines.

The technicians are also responsible for operating and maintaining the laboratory equipment used in manufacturing and packaging the medicines. They monitor the product as it is being produced for quality control purposes so that the medicines that make it to the market are of superior quality. Technicians may also find themselves working in industries other than pharmaceuticals, such as cosmetics, food, plastics, and custom chemicals.

While still in school, students should prepare for a career as a pharmaceutical and medicine manufacturing

Equipment repair, maintenance, and operation are some of the tasks that may be assigned to pharmaceutical manufacturing technicians.

science technician by working in laboratories. They will then become skilled in working with the equipment that medical laboratories use and learn their way around the environment. Today's industrial environment requires technicians to be well trained in state-of-the-art instruments, computer methods, safety protocols, and federal and state government regulations. Most newly hired workers begin as laboratory aides, whose duties include cleaning the tools and equipment.

According to the Office of Science Education in the National Institutes of Health, the fastest employment growth for biological technicians will be seen in pharmaceutical and medicine manufacturing. As a large portion of the population ages, the demand for medication to treat age-related conditions will spike, further ensuring that the industry will stay strong well into the future. Employment opportunities for pharmaceutical and medicine manufacturing science technicians are expected to increase 18 percent by 2018, according to the BLS.

## Quality Control Associate

A quality control (QC) associate carries out testing and analysis to ensure that biomedical research studies and biomedical products meet specifications and regulatory guidelines. QC associates work in quality control laboratories and in biomanufacturing environments. They use complex instrumentation and laboratory equipment to conduct tests and analyses that are used in scientific research studies or to ensure compliance with product quality regulations.

Because the products being developed or manufactured directly impact people's lives, strict FDA regulations must be followed and documented at every step. In the manufacturing of pharmaceutical products, companies are required to follow standard operating procedures, and every step of every process must have a traceable, written record. QC associates are responsible for this documentation. They perform analytical tests, gather and assess data from those tests, and write documentation and reports.

Beyond pharmaceuticals, opportunities for employment as a QC associate are available at agricultural

## THE STEPS OF PROCESSING A PRESCRIPTION

| |
|---|
| 1. Enter prescription order information into the patient's profile. |
| 2. Select appropriate products for dispensing. |
| 3. Obtain pharmaceuticals, medical equipment, devices, and supplies from inventory. |
| 4. Calculate quantity and days supply of finished dosage forms for dispensing. |
| 5. Measure/count quantity of finished dosage forms for dispensing. |
| 6. Process and handle radiopharmaceuticals. |
| 7. Perform calculations for radiopharmaceuticals. |
| 8. Process and handle chemotherapeutic medications commercially available. |
| 9. Perform calculations for oral chemotherapeutic medications. |
| 10. Process and handle investigational products. |
| 11. Package finished dosage forms. |
| 12. Affix labels to containers. |
| 13. Assemble patient information materials, such as drug information sheets, patient package inserts, or HIPAA forms. |
| 14. Check for accuracy during processing of the medication order. |
| 15. Verify the data entry, measurements, preparation, and/or packaging of medications produced by other technicians as allowed by law. |
| 16. Prepare prescription for final check by pharmacist. |

organizations that develop genetically modified foods and at energy companies that are developing and manufacturing cleaner fuels. Opportunities are also available in the chemical industry and in industrial settings where biotechnology is being used to reduce the environmental impact of manufacturing. If interested in becoming a QC associate, you should specialize in agricultural, biotechnology, industrial pharmaceutical, or bioprocess technology during your AAS degree program.

## Process Technicians

Process technicians perform and document the daily manufacturing operations in biomedical, biopharmaceutical, and bioindustrial settings. These individuals operate process equipment in a sterile or clean-room environment. Because there are many different complex steps in biomedical research and biomanufacturing environments, a process technician must be detail-oriented, alert, and thorough.

Process technicians (also referred to as manufacturing associates or operators) need to be proficient with computer and electronic equipment and have an understanding of basic biotechnology processing. A process technician might be involved in mixing and measuring chemicals and reagents to synthesize cell cultures, make finished drugs (capsules, tablets, liquids, or ointments), or perform purification or formulation of complex products. A process technician might also be involved in cleaning and sterilizing production equipment and glassware or in operating the equipment that packages and labels a finished product. Process technicians are required to follow specific safety guidelines and work within Food and Drug Administration requirements.

Process technicians may work for biomedical, biopharmaceutical, and biomanufacturing companies where

As a process technician, you will spend a great deal of time in labs learning everything from how to mix chemicals together safely to how to keep equipment sterile and safe.

products such as vaccines, medicines, enzymes, and cell cultures are created. Opportunities at agricultural, energy, and chemical companies also exist. Many community colleges have created degree and certificate programs designed specifically to prepare individuals for process technician work. These degrees or certificates may be named biowork, biotechnology, bioprocess technology, or industrial pharmaceutical technology.

# Sell, Sell, Sell!

**W**ith an AAS degree, graduates can enter the field of pharmaceutical sales. Pharmaceutical representatives work for drug and supply companies to provide and sell products to doctors' offices and hospitals. There is generally no formal educational requirement for sales representative positions, but many jobs require some postsecondary education. Factors such as communication skills, the ability to sell, and familiarity with brands are essential to being a successful sales representative.

## Course Work

Once enrolled in an AAS degree program, students should specialize in pharmaceutical sales technology and take courses in anatomy and physiology, communications, law, pharmacy practice, medical terminology, pharmacology, sales and marketing, and billing and coding. They should complete formal study in pharmaceutical science topics like drug discoveries and mechanisms, pharmacology,

## TERMS TO KNOW

Any subject is easier to understand, learn, and memorize once you know the basic terms involved. Here are just a few of the terms taught in pharmaceutical-related classes. Take a look at this list. How many of the words do you know already?

**Adulteration:** The mishandling of medication that can lead to contamination/impurity, falsification of contents, or loss of drug quality or potency.

**Analgesic:** A drug given in order to relieve pain.

**Barbiturate:** A drug that acts as a central nervous system depressant, often employed in the treatment of seizures and as a sedative or hypnotic agent.

**Board of pharmacy:** State board regulating the practice of pharmacy within the state.

**Boxed warning:** Drug warning placed in the prescribing information or package insert of a product, indicating a significant risk of potentially dangerous side effects.

**Controlled substance:** Any drug or other substance that is scheduled I through V and regulated by the DEA.

**Drug Enforcement Administration (DEA):** Federal agency within the U.S. Department of Justice that enforces U.S. laws and regulations related to controlled substances.

**Drug Facts and Comparisons:** Reference book found in pharmacies that contains detailed information on medications.

**Food and Drug Administration (FDA):** Federal agency within the U.S. Department of Health and Human Services responsible for assuring the safety, efficacy, and security of human and veterinary drugs, biological products, medical devices, the national food supply, cosmetics, and radioactive products.

**Inpatient pharmacy:** A pharmacy in a hospital or institutional setting.

**Material safety data sheet (MSDS):** A document providing chemical product information.

**Medicaid:** Federal and state-operated insurance program covering health care costs and prescription drugs for low-income children, adults, the elderly, and the disabled.

**Medicare:** Federal and state-managed insurance program covering health care costs and prescription drugs for individuals older than sixty-five years old or younger with long-term disabilities.

**Medicine:** The science and art dealing with health maintenance; the prevention, alleviation, or cure of disease; or the easing of pain or discomfort.

**Misbranding:** Labeling a product in a way that is false or misleading.

**Opioid:** Any agent that binds to opioid receptors.

**Opium:** An analgesic that is made from the poppy plant.

**Outpatient pharmacy:** Pharmacy serving

**Pharmaceuticals:** Prescription medicine made from plant and chemical-based compounds.

**Pharmacist:** Person who dispenses drugs and counsels patients on medication use and any interactions they may have with food or other drugs.

**Pharmacy:** Place where drugs are sold.

**Pharmacy clerk:** Person who assists the pharmacist at the front counter of the pharmacy and often accepts payment for medications.

**Pharmacy Technician Certification Board (PTCB):** Organization that issues a national exam for pharmacy technicians.

dosage principles, and regulatory measures. Internships also allow students to explore the pharmaceutical industry firsthand, offering them laboratory training or experience in drug manufacturing and distribution.

Once you've graduated, you will find a highly competitive job market. Each job opening typically receives hundreds of applicants. One of the keys is networking and using your contacts—friends, neighbors, teachers, advisers, parents, your doctor—to get an "in" with someone in a hiring position within a pharmaceutical company. Some companies will want sales reps who have a bachelor's degree or a master's in business administration (MBA) and some expertise in chemistry, biology, pharmaceutical science, pharmacology, nursing, biomedical sciences, or sales and marketing. Others, however, will hire someone with an AAS who is confident, positive, and persuasive; has great interpersonal skills; is willing to learn; and is a "quick study." Most importantly, you must have a true interest in and aptitude for science.

## Certification Programs

To boost your qualifications and stand out from the crowd of applicants, you may choose to acquire the certified sales professional designation through the Manufacturers' Representatives Educational Research Foundation (MRERF). The certification process involves three days of intensive seminars that discuss managing stress, maintaining a positive attitude, learning the selling process, and practicing general business skills.

The National Association of Pharmaceutical Representatives (NAPRx) also offers a certification option

Being a sales rep is an exciting and dynamic job—which is why you will face stiff competition when you start job hunting. Be ready to show your strengths as a salesperson and separate yourself from the crowd.

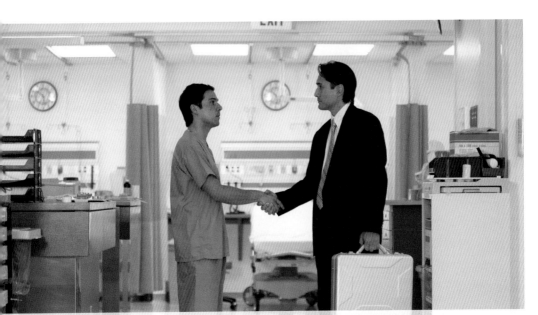

The field of medicine is growing so quickly and expanding in so many different directions that sales representatives must be even more aware than doctors of the latest research and products. In fact, salespeople are the ones who often educate and inform doctors about the newest, most effective medicines and treatments.

that bestows the title of certified national pharmaceutical representative (CNPR) upon recipients. The certification, which requires the successful completion of a multiple-choice examination, allows you to apply for entry-level pharmaceutical sales rep positions.

Certificate programs like these will offer instruction in understanding industry regulations, recognizing important pharmaceutical terms, applying selling techniques, and coordinating with government agencies like Medicare. A certificate program can also enhance your selling skills in a hospital setting by providing instruction on how to use sales materials and follow all hospital drug-sampling regulations.

## The Nature of the Work

Pharmaceutical representatives work for drug and supply companies to provide and sell products to doctors' offices and hospitals. New hires receive intense sales and product training. Once trained, a pharmaceutical representative will have the job of selling the company's products to a variety of sources. In a typical day, a pharmaceutical sales rep makes several calls and/or presentations to hospitals, health maintenance organizations (HMOs), doctors' offices, and pharmacies. Much of the job is spent traveling, locally or beyond, because representatives must remain in direct contact with the locations to which they sell.

Sales reps must work constantly to create, maintain, and expand sales in a designated territory and provide continuing education and service to targeted physicians. Sales reps must be self-starters and be able to work independently, setting their own goals and doing what it takes to meet them. In order to work as a pharmaceutical rep, you'll need to have detailed knowledge of the product you're selling and demonstrate strong communication skills when meeting with customers.

You'll also need to be both patient and persuasive with your clients, since some sales are more difficult, complicated, and time-consuming to make than others. Some clients will need to be convinced that your product is superior in some way to the one they are already using, and this can take lots of explanation, education, patience, and skill.

# Chapter 5

# Behind the Scenes and Out in Front

**W**hile pharmacy technicians, manufacturing technicians, and sales reps make up the majority of pharmaceutical jobs available to those with AAS degrees, certifications, or less than two years of study, there are still some other employment options. Some are behind the scenes, while others are right out in front of the public, and some require more education and training than others.

## *Pharmacy Billing Specialists*

Pharmacy billing specialists are responsible for the timely and accurate submission of invoices to the customer or patient for all services and products provided. They are also responsible for follow-up with the customer or patient to ensure the receipt of on-time and in-full payments. They must evaluate all payments received and properly apply the payment to the correct patient or customer account. They must determine quantities and prices for drugs billed and verify that services and products are correctly authorized and that the required documentation is on file.

The documentation and paperwork associated with the pharmaceutical field require attention to detail, accuracy, organizational skill, and facility with data entry and record keeping.

Pharmacy billing specialists must verify that payments received are correct according to the fee schedule, and they must notify management when overpayments and/or duplicate payments for services are received. They must communicate to the patient or customer when his or her insurance carrier fails to make payments within the agreed upon timeframe or will not cover certain medicines.

In addition to an AAS degree, those seeking employment as a pharmacy billing specialist should have experience in computer application software and medical billing technical training.

# CREATING A RÉSUMÉ

What should you include in your résumé when applying for a job in the pharmaceutical field? Start with the basics: name, address, phone number, and e-mail address. Next, highlight the education you have had, whether it is a certification program, online program, or an associate's degree. Mention courses, degrees, certifications, special workshops, or any relevant background. If you know scores or grades, you can include them, and you can also list the curriculum that you covered, including (depending on the job in question):

- Medical and pharmaceutical terminology
- Pharmacology of medications
- Retail pharmacy procedures
- Medicare and Medicaid reimbursements
- Pharmaceutical calculations
- FDA drug safety guidelines
- Pharmacy practice ethics
- Prescription filling
- Medication compounding
- Basic anatomy
- Patient care and interaction
- Medication inventory management
- Sales and Marketing
- Billing and record keeping
- Manufacturing processes
- Quality control and assurance
- Industrial safety
- Research and development
- Standard operating procedures and federal regulations

## Pharmacy Records Manager

Retail and hospital pharmacies contain hundreds, or even thousands, of computerized and paper files containing patient information. It is the pharmacy records manager's job to effectively and efficiently organize, file, and maintain all of these records. Pharmacy records managers organize and manage health information data by ensuring its quality, accuracy, accessibility, and security in both paper and electronic systems. They use various classification systems to code and categorize patient information for reimbursement purposes, for databases and registries, and to maintain patients' medical and treatment histories.

The records manager must decide what filing system to use, whether alphabetical (by patient last name) or numeric (in which each patient is assigned a random number). A records management software package must be selected and implemented to keep tabs on patients and their prescriptions, to allow a pharmacy to accept electronic information from doctors and their staff, and to furnish a drug database that lists all the drugs available in the pharmacy and information about potentially dangerous drug interactions.

Records managers must also establish an effective channel of communications so that surgeons, pharmacy administrators, and pharmacy technicians work together to double-check the accuracy of both computerized and handwritten medical records. They must ensure that files are stored in the proper location so that they can be located quickly in case of a medical or other emergency.

Keeping track of every single person's medical history and records is a demanding job that requires managers who are comfortable with handling piles of paperwork, as well as flipping back and forth between hard copies and computer software to double-check facts and figures.

They must guarantee that records are not handled improperly, shared with anyone other than patient-approved doctors and medical personnel, or removed from the pharmacy without explicit permission and instructions from a doctor or pharmacy supervisor. The confidentiality and security of patient records and prescription history must be preserved at all costs.

In addition to an AAS degree, many employers will require professional certification before hiring someone as a records manager.

## Pharmacy Clerk

Pharmacy clerks, also known as pharmacy aides, perform many of the administrative duties in a pharmacy. This includes answering phones, accepting prescriptions, filing records, and receiving payment from customers. They serve as cashiers much of the time, so they need good customer service skills and a facility with cash registers and transaction processing. Clerks do not actually dispense medications, but they do process customer payments for medication. They assist in most other areas of pharmacy work. Clerks work under the supervision of pharmacists and pharmacy technicians.

No formal training or education is needed to become a pharmacy clerk. In fact, it is possible to be hired as a pharmacy clerk right out of high school. The necessary skills are acquired through on-the-job training. However, you might still choose to enroll in a pharmacy clerk training program at a community college or adult education center. Such programs cover basic administration skills, as well as pharmacy terminology and procedures. With enough training and experience, pharmacy clerks may even be able to advance to a management or supervisory position at a pharmacy.

## Chapter 6

# Acing the Interview, Getting the Job

**Y**ou have learned a lot of information and now it is time to apply all of it to getting a job in the pharmacy field. The job interview is extremely important. It is often the key to whether or not you spend days or weeks—or many months—searching for a job. Preparing for the interview takes effort and practice, but it will pay off when you are the one who gets hired! What do you need to know?

## Preparing for the Interview

Get ready for your job interview by choosing what to wear, mapping out the route to the location, and leaving early. Be sure to wear something professional, such as a suit and tie for men, and dress pants or a skirt and jacket for women. Sherry Maysonave, head of Empowerment Enterprises, an image consulting firm in Texas, told *Forbes* magazine, "That first impression on an interview counts so much, and you don't want to be out of the race before the interview even begins. That [first impression] happens in less than thirty seconds and is based entirely upon your attire," she adds.

Experts suggest women avoid open-toe shoes, sleeveless tops, jangling jewelry, "in your face" designer labels, and strong perfumes/colognes. Other suggestions include minimal makeup, neatly brushed hair, and polished shoes. Maysonave explains, "Your interview attire indicates your socio-economic status, and it can actually impact your salary offer. If someone looks like they need a job, they are probably not going to get it," she adds. "And they are definitely not going to get the same offer that someone with a polished look will."

In addition to dressing appropriately, map out the route you will take to get to the interview, and leave early in case of traffic or other complications. If you are taking public transportation, be even more vigilant about having enough time. Buses and trains often run late or get delayed along the way.

First impressions have a powerful influence and are impossible to erase once made. Double-check your wardrobe and see which outfit is most likely to say, "I'm a talented professional."

# MAKING THE MOST OF JOB FAIRS

**Job fairs can be a great way to find open positions in the pharmaceutical field. Knowing how to work a job fair before you attend one can make the experience more effective and efficient. Here are tips to keep in mind when you head to a job fair:**

1. Pre-register if possible.
2. Research the participating companies that will be there.
3. Develop a list of questions to ask employers.
4. Proofread your résumé and make multiple copies.
5. Dress nicely. You are making an important first impression.
6. Take time to talk to representatives instead of just dropping off your résumé. Make an impression that they will remember.
7. Use your manners: "Please," "Thank you," and "You're welcome" are polite and memorable.
8. Prepare a thirty-second introduction that conveys your name, expertise, and why you want to work with this particular company.
9. Practice what you want to say so that it will come out smoothly and confidently.
10. Greet with a strong handshake and maintain eye contact.
11. Take notes on whom you talked to and which companies they represented.

12. Ask representatives for their business cards and use the contact information to send thank-you notes after the job fair.

**What about once the job fair is over? How do you follow up appropriately? According to Karen E. Lamb, assistant director of career advising and curriculum at Arizona State University, "Once a personal connection has been made, follow up by sending an e-mail, business letter, or handwritten note that highlights your qualifications, emphasizes your interest in the job, and expresses your appreciation for their consideration. This kind of follow-up, immediately following the job fair, is an excellent way to distinguish your-self from the other participants at the event—and stand out in the crowd."**

## During the Interview

During the interview, make sure to:

- Arrive on time
- Say "please" and "thank you"
- Maintain eye contact
- Use proper body language

Although each employer is going to be slightly different, some questions are commonly asked by most interviewers. Knowing how to answer each one of them is important. Practice your answers at home first so that you can deliver them smoothly and confidently during the actual interview. Here are some of the most typical questions you might be asked:

- *Why do you think you are a good fit for this job?* The employer is looking for solid character traits like professionalism, dependability, punctuality, and attention to detail. Be specific.

- *Describe the most difficult customer service experience you've had and how you handled the situation.* Talk about your ability to be both flexible and patient. Give an example of how you have handled challenging customers in the past, but show that you kept your cool.

- *Tell us about your prior work experience.* Discuss your organizational skills and ability to multitask.

- *Are you ready to take a screening exam?* Even if you are certified, some employers may also insist on an additional exam. It will assess your ability to measure dosage, understand common pharmacy procedures, and follow state regulations.

- *Tell me about yourself.* Connect personal information to why you want a career in pharmacy.

Practicing the answers to some of the most commonly asked questions can help you calm your nerves and project a confident attitude during the actual interview—even if you're still nervous on the inside.

- *Why should I hire you?*

Highlight your education and training, and show what makes you unique. If you have any special talents on the computer or if you speak multiple languages, this is the time to mention it.

- *What are your major weaknesses?*

Be honest, but find a way to put a positive spin on the flaw.

- *Where do you see yourself in two, three, or five years?*

Show that you have some plans for the future, including a desire to look into different career pathways in the pharmaceutical industry and additional job-related course work, training, and/or certifications.

- *How do you spend your free time?*

This question reveals a little bit more about you on a personal level. This is a good place to mention your volunteering experiences, for example.

- *Do you have any questions for me?*

Always have questions because it shows you are interested and have been paying close attention. Don't ask about your days off or future vacation time. Instead, ask about details of the position, as well as when you might hear back from them regarding whether or not you are hired.

## After the Interview

After the interview, be sure to send either a thank-you note in the mail or an e-mail. Thank the interviewer for his or her time and the chance to work with the company in the near future. Add that you will be waiting to hear from them. If the date they gave you for letting you know comes and goes and you haven't heard anything, you should feel comfortable making a simple follow-up phone call to inquire about the status of the open position.

# Chapter 7

# You Got the Job! What's Next?

**T**he learning, studying, focusing, and working have all paid off! You have a job in the pharmaceutical field, and it is everything you had imagined it would be. You are learning something new every day and proving to your coworkers that you are the right person for the job. So. . .now what? What should your next career goals be? There are quite a few you can add to your list.

## *Being an Asset*

Doing your job well is important, of course. But just doing the basics is not enough. High-quality and highly valued workers have to go beyond this. Start by establishing good work habits. This means:

- Arriving to work on time
- Not leaving until you are supposed to
- Stepping in to help fellow workers even if not asked or expected to
- Following directions carefully

Doing your job is not always enough. To make a positive impression on your boss and coworkers, go that extra mile and do more than the minimum expected of you. You have the job—now it's time to shine and show that you are ready and able for more!

- Making quality customer service a priority
- Thinking and speaking positively
- Talking respectfully to your coworkers
- Being neat and clean
- Avoiding procrastination
- Volunteering for assignments

The employee who always goes the extra mile, who volunteers for projects and makes a special effort, and who works as part of a team is a valued one. You can be that employee!

Ideally, learning never stops. Pursuing additional education not only meets state requirements but also makes you a more valuable and skilled employee.

## Getting Additional Education

Many of the pharmaceutical jobs discussed here require additional hours of education every few years in order for one's certification to be updated and renewed. A number of different companies and colleges offer this type of training. Some of the training can be done online, while other hours may be offered through your workplace. Information is provided in live presentations, correspondence courses, workshops, in-service training programs, journal articles, and audio or video recordings. Some

# MEETING TWO PHARMACY TECHS

Meet Krystal. She is twenty-four and lives in northwest Oregon. After high school, she knew she wanted a career in the health field, but she wasn't sure in exactly which sector. After seeing a commercial on television, she decided to pursue a job as a pharmacy tech. After attending school in Spokane, Washington, she was hired by Walgreens. She is now the senior technician and says her job involves "customer service, taking in and typing new prescriptions, doing insurance billing, scheduling, ordering, doing inventory, filling prescriptions, and assisting the pharmacist."

Krystal's favorite parts of the job are being able to help people and learning new things about medications. She sometimes struggles with billing insurance and having to work weekends. "It takes a thick-skinned person to be able to work in pharmacy," she says. "It is guaranteed you will be yelled at once a day, and you have to be understanding and extremely patient. You deal with lots of customers who are sick or coming in for a sick child," she adds. "People won't always have the money for medications they or a family member needs, and you have to do your very best to help each and every person, no matter what the situation." Krystal is hoping to start college within a year to become a veterinarian. She knows that her time spent as a pharmacy technician gets her one step closer to that goal.

Michelle is twenty-two and lives in New Jersey. She worked in a store that also included a pharmacy. When the pharmacist needed a new tech, he asked Michelle to take the job, primarily because of her outgoing nature with customers and solid work ethic. She has been working as a tech for almost three years now and says her favorite part of the job is knowing the regulars. "Personally knowing my customers completely changes my work environment," she says. "I hold memories I never want to forget."

Like most techs, Michelle spends a great deal of time typing and filling prescriptions, answering the phone, and ringing up patients. Recently, she helped with a big store cleanup. "It included changing ceiling tiles and cleaning every inch of the pharmacy," she explains. "I've cleaned things I didn't even know existed!"

Michelle is not planning to pursue an advanced health care degree. In fact, she is an art student. She advises young people to look into a pharmacy tech job. "I have learned a lot of life skills from working in the pharmacy," she says. "I understand how important it is to take opportunities because there is always something to be learned from them. I would never take back any of my experiences here."

courses have a fee, but a number of online courses are free. In addition, workers can take additional course work in order to achieve certification in a new area or specialty or begin work toward a bachelor's or master's degree in order to expand their career options.

## Keeping Your Options Open

Brieanna is twenty-four and lives on the East Coast. She is currently attending Seton Hall University in South Orange, New Jersey, to earn her bachelor's degree in nursing. First, however, she earned an AAS degree. She originally worked the customer service desk in a pharmacy but eventually wanted a "change of scenery." After a combination of on-the-job training, studying, and taking the state test, Brieanna became a certified pharmacy technician.

Three years later, Brieanna loves her job. "The best part of the job is that it is personal," she says. She found she became quite close to her customers over time. "You begin to know what their health history is, plus personal history, and current situations," she continues. "At the end of the day, there is that trusting relationship, as you know people count on you for their medication, as well as to listen if they want to ramble about something going on at home or at work." Naturally, Brieanna encounters less pleasant aspects of her profession, too. "I dislike it when people write fraudulent scripts [prescriptions]," she explains. "Narcotics is a big issue in today's world, and I think it is rapidly growing instead of being controlled. "

Like most pharmacy techs, Brieanna spends her day typing and filling prescriptions, handling the register, doing daily counts of medications, keeping the pharmacy clean, filling supplies, and handling insurance claims. She advises young people who are interested in the profession to do as much hands-on training as possible. She adds, "I think, in order to be fit for this job, you must be very organized, neat, able and willing to keep a trustful relationship with customers, and successfully convert the day's supply and amount of medication." Her final advice to those considering a career as a pharmacy technician: "This is a very enjoyable job for anyone who is personable and willing to learn new things. The health care field is always evolving, and there will be new drugs, new recommendations, and new things to learn. Keep information confidential, and keep an open mind!"

## Finding a Mentor

If you've had mentors as you were growing up—like teachers, guidance counselors, bosses or managers, religious leaders, or neighbors—you already know how helpful they can be. They can connect you with resources, teach you important lessons, give you advice, serve as a role model, and make learning more fun. Finding a mentor when you are just starting out in the pharmaceuticals field can bear similar fruit. Mentors can not only help you make sure you earn any certificates or degrees you want and need, they can also connect you with professional organizations and programs.

Brian Kurth, author of *Test-Drive Your Dream Job: A Step-by-Step Guide to Finding and Creating the Work You Love*, says, "Perhaps the most important step in pursuing a dream job is to find someone who already works in that field who can offer guidance and advice as you proceed. Believe it or not," he continues, "this is not as difficult as it might sound. In my experience, many people express fear at the prospect of asking for help from a prospective mentor. Why would they want to help you, after all? The answer is easy: people like helping other people! By asking a prospective mentor for help," Kurth adds, "they are being told they are admired for what they do, their career is in demand, and their experiences and insights are valuable to others. Not everyone will see it this way, but once you start asking, you'll be surprised how receptive people are."

In an article for *Forbes*, author Kerry Hannon says you should also make the idea of mentoring sound like fun. "When asking, don't make it sound like work. Exude a sense of excitement. Smile and laugh a little.

Finding the right mentor in the pharmacy field can be a crucial step in determining where you want to go next in the field and how you will get there.

Mentorship and sponsorship are energy-boosting opportunities for both of you, and it often turns into a friendship. Find ways to meet regularly, even without an urgent agenda. Nurture the relationship," advises Hannon.

Becoming an asset to your employer, whether it be in a hospital, clinic, drugstore, or other setting, is not only what helps ensure job security but also makes you a more skilled, ethical, and respected employee. If you apply the same time, enthusiasm, and effort that you applied to *becoming* a terrific employee to actually *being* a terrific employee, you are sure to create a win-win situation for everyone. You will be putting yourself on the road to professional advancement, success, and fulfillment.

**accredited**  Describes an authorized educational institution.

**adverse reaction**  A harmful and undesired effect resulting from a medication.

**chemotherapeutic**  A drug used in chemotherapy treatment.

**compounding**  Mixing or combining ingredients.

**congestion**  Excessive fluid and swelling in the sinuses.

**decongestant**  A medicine that helps lesson congestion.

**dosage**  The size and frequency of a dose, or suggested intake, of medicine.

**drug compliance**  The degree to which a patient correctly follows medical advice.

**efficacy**  Ability to produce a desired or intended result.

**expectorant**  A medicine promoting the opening of air passages, such as in the lungs.

**HIPAA**  The Health Insurance Portability and Accountability Act of 1996, designed to maintain the privacy and security of people's health information.

**investigation product**  A pharmaceutical product that has been recalled.

**pharmacology**  The branch of medicine concerned with the uses, effects, and modes of drugs.

**radiopharmaceutical**  A radioactive compound used for diagnosing medical conditions.

**transcriptionist**  A person who turns oral medical reports into written notes.

Accreditation Council for Pharmacy Education (ACPE)
135 South LaSalle Street, Suite 4100
Chicago, IL 60603-4810
(312) 664-3575
Web site: https://www.acpe-accredit.org
ACPE is the national agency for the accreditation of
    professional degree programs in pharmacy and pro-
    viders of continuing pharmacy education.

American Association of Pharmacy Technicians (AAPT)
P.O .Box 1447
Greensboro, NC 27402
(877) 368-4771
Web site: http://www.pharmacytechnician.com
The AAPT promotes the safe, efficacious, and cost
    effective dispensing, distribution, and use of medica-
    tions. It also provides continuing education
    programs and services to help technicians update
    their skills to keep pace with changes in pharmacy
    services.

Canadian Pharmacists Association
1785 Alta Vista Drive
Ottawa, ON K1G 3Y6
Canada
(800) 917-9489, ext. 501
Web site: http://www.pharmacists.ca
The Canadian Pharmacists Association advocates for
    pharmacists and supports its members to advance the
    profession and enhance patient outcomes.

National Association of Boards of Pharmacy (NABP)
1600 Feehanville Drive
Mount Prospect, IL 60056
(847) 391-4406
Web site: http://www.nabp.net
The NABP is an impartial professional organization that
supports the state boards of pharmacy in creating
uniform regulations to protect public health.

National Association of Pharmaceutical Representatives
(NAPRx)
2020 Pennsylvania Avenue NW, Suite 5050
Washington, DC 20006-1811
(800) 284-1060
The NAPRx is the largest trade association for sales reps,
sales managers, and sales trainers who work in the
pharmaceutical industry. It is widely known for its
CNPR Certification Training Program, which provides
vocational education for individuals looking to enter a
pharmaceutical sales career.

National Pharmacy Technician Association (NPTA)
P.O. Box 683148
Houston, TX 77268
(888) 247-8700
Web site: http://www.pharmacytechnician.org
The NPTA is the world's largest professional organization
established specifically for pharmacy technicians. It
is dedicated to advancing the value of pharmacy
technicians and the vital roles they play in pharmaceutical care.

Pharmacy Technician Certification Board (PTCB)
2215 Constitution Avenue NW
Washington, DC 20037
(800) 363-8012
Web site: http://www.ptcb.org
The PTCB develops, maintains, promotes, and administers
   a nationally accredited certification and recertification
   program for pharmacy technicians to enable the most
   effective support of pharmacists to advance patient safety.

Rx&D Canada's Research-Based Pharmaceutical
   Companies
55 Metcalfe Street, Suite 1220
Ottawa, ON K1P 6L5
Canada
(800) 363-0203
Web site: http://www.canadapharma.org
Rx&D is the association of leading research-based pharmaceutical companies dedicated to improving the
   health of Canadians through the discovery and development of new medicines and vaccines.

## Web Sites

Due to the changing nature of Internet links, Rosen
Publishing has developed an online list of Web sites
related to the subject of this book. This site is updated
regularly. Please use this link to access the list:

http://www.rosenlinks.com/HCC/Pharm

Barker, Geoff. *Health and Social Care Careers*. Mankato, MN: AMICUS, 2011.

Brezina, Corona. *Getting a Job in Health Care* (Job Basics: Getting the Job You Need). New York, NY: Rosen Publishing, 2014.

Carroll, Jamuna. *The Pharmaceutical Industry*. Farmington Hills, MI: Greenhaven Press, 2008.

Engdahl, Sylvia. *Prescription Drugs*. Farmington Hills, MI: Greenhaven Press, 2008.

Freeman, Brian. *The Ultimate Guide to Choosing a Medical Specialty*. 3rd ed. New York, NY: McGraw-Hill, 2013.

Harmon, Daniel J. *New Medicines: Issues of Approval, Access, and Product Safety*. New York, NY: Rosen Publishing, 2009.

Leonard, Basia. *The Truth About Prescription Drugs*. New York, NY: Rosen Publishing, 2011.

Miller, Malinda. *The Pharmaceutical Industry: Better Medicine for the 21st Century*. Broomall, PA: Mason Crest Publishers, 2010.

Moini, Jahangir. *Pocket Guide for Pharmacy Technicians*. Farmington Hills, MI: Delmar Learning, 2013.

Olive, M. Foster. *Prescription Pain Relievers*. New York, NY: Chelsea House Publishers, 2005.

Peterson's. *Vocational & Technical Schools East: More Than 2,300 Vocational Schools East of the Mississippi River* (Peterson's Vocational and Technical Schools East). Lawrenceville, NJ: Peterson's, 2009.

Peterson's. *Vocational & Technical Schools West: More Than 2,300 Vocational Schools West of the Mississippi River* (Peterson's Vocational and Technical Schools West). Lawrenceville, NJ: Peterson's, 2009.

Ruschmann, Paul. *Prescription and Non-Prescription Drugs.* New York, NY: Chelsea House Publishers, 2007.

Shatkin, Laurence, and Michael Farr. *Top 100 Careers Without a Four-Year Degree.* Indianapolis, IN: JIST Works, 2012.

Webster, LiAnne. *Pharmacy Practice Today for the Pharmacy Technician: Career Training for the Pharmacy Technician.* Philadelphia, PA: Mosby, 2013.

Wilson, Patrick. *Health IT JumpStart: The Best First Step Toward an IT Career in Health Information Technology.* Indianapolis, IN: John Wiley & Sons, Inc., 2012.

Wischnitzer, Saul, and Edith Wischnitzer. *Top 100 Health-Care Careers: Your Complete Guidebook to Training and Jobs in Allied Health, Nursing, Medicine, and More.* 3rd ed. Indianapolis, IN: JIST Works, 2011.

Zott, Lynn. *Prescription Drug Abuse.* Farmington Hills, MI: Greenhaven Press, 2013.

AboutBioScience.org. "Process Technician." Retrieved March 2013 (http://www.aboutbioscience.org /careers/processtechnician).

AboutBioScience.org. "Quality Control Associate." Retrieved March 2013 (http://www.aboutbioscience .org/careers/qualitycontrolassociate).

American Medical Association. *Health Care Careers Directory 2011–2012*. 39th ed. Chicago, IL: American Medical Association, 2011.

AssociatesDegree.com. "Pharmaceutical and Medicine Manufacturing Science Technician." Retrieved March 2013 (http://www.associatesdegree.com/best-jobs /health-care/pharmaceutical-and-medicine -manufacturing-science-technician).

Bourne, Leah. "The Perfect Interview Outfit." Forbes.com, July 30, 2009. Retrieved March 2013 (http://www .forbes.com/2009/07/30/interview-outfit-fashion -forbes-woman-style-budget.html).

Boyce, Brienna. E-mail interview with author, March 23, 2013.

Damp, Dennis V. *Health Care Job Explosion! High Growth Health Care Careers and Job Locators*. McKees Rocks, PA: Bookhaven Press LLC, 2006.

Deeds, Krystal. E-mail interview with author, March 24, 2013.

Education Portal. "Billing Specialist: Salary, Requirements, and Career Information." Retrieved March 2013 (http://education-portal.com/articles/Billing_Specialist _Salary_Requirements_and_Career_Information.html).

Education Portal. "Pharmacy Clerk Jobs: Career Options, Duties, and Requirements." Retrieved March 2013 (http://education-portal.com/articles/Pharmacy_Clerk _Jobs_Career_Options_Duties_and_Requirements.html).

EmploymentGuide.com. "Making the Most of Job Fairs."
Retrieved March 2013 (http://www.employmentguide
.com/careeradvice/Making_the_Most_of_Job_Fairs.html).

Ferguson. *The Top 100: The Fastest-Growing Careers for the
21st Century.* 5th ed. New York, NY: Facts On File, 2011.

Fowler, Garth. "Making the Most of Career Fairs."
*Science Careers*, December 9, 2005. Retrieved
March 2013 (http://sciencecareers.sciencemag.org
/career_magazine/previous_issues/articles/2005_12_09
/nodoi.15291115422083250132).

Fry, Kellie. "Interview Like a Pro: How to Land Your
Pharmacy Technician Dream Job!" *MK Education*,
February 17, 2011. Retrieved March 2013 (http://
blog.mkedu.org/bid/56822/Interview-Like-a-Pro
-How-to-Land-Your-Pharmacy-Technician-Dream-Job).

Hannon, Kerry. "How to Find a Mentor." Forbes.com,
October 31, 2011. Retrieved March 2013 (http://
www.forbes.com/sites/kerryhannon/2011/10/31
/how-to-find-a-mentor).

Illich, Stan. "Pharmacy Technician Job Interviewing Tips."
PharmTech Pros, 2013. Retrieved March 2013
(http://www.pharmacytechpros.com/pharmacy
-technician-job-interviewing-tips.html).

Kasson, Elisabeth Greenbaum. "How to Prep for a
Pharmacy Tech Interview." PharmTech Pros, April 8,
2011. Retrieved March 2013 (http://career-news
.healthcallings.com/2011/04/08/how-to-prep
-for-a-pharmacy-tech-interview).

Kasson, Elisabeth Greenbaum. "Interview Questions for
Pharmacy Techs." Health Callings, November 29,
2012. Retrieved March 2013 (http://career-news

.healthcallings.com/2012/11/29/interview-questions
-for-pharmacy-techs).

Kirdahy, Matthew. "How to Make the Most of a Career
Fair." Forbes.com, March 27, 2008. Retrieved March
2013 (http://www.forbes.com/2008/03/27/
workplace-jobs-fair-lead-careers-cx_mk_0327career
.html).

Kurth, Brian. "Test-Drive Your Dream Job: A Step-by-Step
Guide to Finding and Creating the Work You Love."
Business Plus, 2008. Retrieved March 2013 (http://
jobsearch.about.com/od/careeradviceresources/a
/career-mentor.htm).

Lamb, Karen E. "Job Hunt: Making the Most of Job Fairs."
ABC15.com, February 9, 2011. Retrieved March
2013 (http://www.abc15.com/dpp/news/region
_southeast_valley/tempe/job-hunt:-making-the
-most-of-job-fairs).

Massimilla, Michelle. E-mail interview with author, March
25, 2013.

Moro, Marianne. "How to Maintain Hospital Pharmacy
Records." eHow.com. Retrieved March 2013 (http://
www.ehow.com/how_7343994_maintain-hospital
-pharmacy-records.html).

National Association of Boards of Pharmacy.
"Technicians." Retrieved March 2013 (http://www
.nabp.net/programs/cpe-monitor/cpe-monitor
-service/technicians).

RTC.edu. "Pharmacy Technician Course Requirements."
Retrieved March 2013 (http://www.rtc.edu
/programs/trainingprograms/pharmacytech
/curriculum.aspx).

Stratford, S. J. *Ferguson Field Guides to Finding a New Career: Health Care.* New York, NY: Checkmark Books, 2009.

Trade-Schools.net. "Pharmacy Career Information." Retrieved March 2013 (http://www.trade-schools .net/career-counselor/pharmacy-technician -information.asp).

Tronshaw, Dubria. "Tips on Taking the Pharmacy Technician Certification Examination." Demand Media. Retrieved March 2013 (http://work.chron .com/tips-taking-pharmacy-technician-certification -examination-16088.html).

VGM editors. *Resumes for Health and Medical Careers.* 3rd ed. Chicago, IL: VGM Career Books, 2004.

Walgreens. "Internships/Programs." 2013. Retrieved March 2013 (http://careers.walgreens.com /students/internships-programs/Default.aspx).

Webb, Michael. E-mail interview with author, March 10, 2013.

Webster, Lianne. E-mail interview with author, March 21, 2013.

Ydoyaga, Shannon. E-mail interview with author, March 18, 2013.

# INDEX

## About the Author

Tamra Orr is the author of many career- and health-related books. She is a graduate of Ball State University. Orr lives in the Pacific Northwest with her family, cat, and dog. She loves to read, write, and go camping. She knows her local pharmacy technicians by name and is grateful for their help every time she stops in to get prescriptions refilled.

## Photo Credits